Just Passing By

The woods are lovely, dark and deep,
But I have promises to keep,
And miles to go before I sleep,
And miles to go before I sleep.

~ Robert Frost

Also by Kamal Parmar

Still Waters 2020
Letters to a son and a daughter 2019
On wings of Time: Poems selected and new 2016
Fleeting Shadows 2010
In the rising mist 2013
Filigree and Flint 1998

Just Passing By

Kamal Parmar

Silver Bow Publishing
720 Sixth Street, Box # 5
New Westminster, BC
CANADA

Title: Just Passing By
Author: Kamal Parmar
Cover Painting: "The High Road and the Path Not Taken"
             by Candice James & Hermine Weiss
                (aka Purple Flame)
Cover Design: Candice James
Editing and Layout: Candice James

All rights reserved including the right to reproduce or translate this book or any portions thereof, in any form except for the use of short passages for review purposes, no part of this book may be reproduced, in part or in whole, or transmitted in any form or by any means, electronically or mechanically, including photocopying, recording, or any information or storage retrieval system without prior permission in writing from the publisher or a license from the Canadian Copyright Collective Agency (Access Copyright)

ISBN: 9781774032411 (print)
ISBN: 9781774032428 (e-book)
© 2022 Silver Bow Publishing

Library and Archives Canada Cataloguing in Publication

Title: Just passing by / Kamal Parmar.
Names: Parmar, Kamal, 1953- author.
Description: Poems.
Identifiers: Canadiana (print) 20220430764 | Canadiana (ebook) 20220430799 | ISBN 9781774032411
  (softcover) | ISBN 9781774032428 (Kindle)
Classification: LCC PS8631.A765 J87 2022 | DDC C811/.6—dc23

info@silverbowpublishing.com
www.silverbowpublishing.com

Just Passing By

"Live in each season as it passes;
breathe the air, drink the drink, taste the fruit,
and resign yourself to the influence of the earth."

— Henry David Thoreau

∞∞∞

" Within you there is a stillness
and a sanctuary
to which you can retreat
at any time and be yourself."

— Hermann Hesse

Just Passing By

Dedication

To all those who have travelled
the winding road of Life's journey.

To all those who cannot find
the missing pieces of the Puzzle.

Acknowledgement

Having an idea and turning it into a book is as hard as it sounds. The experience is both internally challenging and rewarding. More rewarding than I could ever have imagined None of this would have been possible without my family who always stood by me, during those long hours of writing and rewriting, till it took the shape of this book.

I want to thank God, most of all, because without Him I wouldn't have been able to do any of this.

Just Passing By

Contents

Just passing by / 11
Autumn magic / 12
Tread softly / 13
All is not quiet / 14
A musical interlude / 15
A break in the clouds / 16
A park comes alive / 17
An unforgettable summer day / 18
Unfaded memories / 19
Ocean-scape / 21
Spring rain / 22
In the stillness of the night / 23
Almost midnight / 24
After the rain / 25
Not quite dawn / 26
Sounds of summer / 27
Is it Fall? / 28
Still Autumn / 29
Shimmering brook / 30
Sauntering in the forest / 31
Dawn awaits / 32
The early hour / 33
Winter beckons / 35
Sounds of silence / 36
Au revoir / 38
A night to remember / 39
Frayed memories / 40
Resilience / 42
Water's edge / 44
The path still untrodden / 45
Silence speaks / 47
The ebb and tide of memories / 48
The magic hour / 49
Flying high / 50

A pond comes alive / 52
What does a mountain say? / 55
There was a time / 57
Sleeping under the stars / 58
Blue on blue / 61
Passing by—a detour / 63

Author Profile / 65

Just passing by

Under a canopy of fir and spruce,
A path meanders, threading the way,
stitching the forest together.
I inhale the pine-scented air, fill my lungs ...
look up.

A blue cloud-mottled sky squints at me,
peeping through the shaggy headed cedar
and the blossoming dogwood.

In the distance lies the jagged line of cypress,
ancient emblems so sacred
that speak of days of yore,
when our ancestors walked this earth
and ceremonies were held
under their sacred boughs,
while the forest echoed with the sound of drums.

I run my fingers over
the mossy gnarled bark of the aspen,
it speaks volumes though its tongue is muted.
In the hushed silence , louder than words,
your voice rises like a psalm dissolving into the air.

Wild blueberries compete with gooseberries
to straddle the damp floor
matted with ferns and hemlocks
to cast dappled shadows across the pathway.

A bird calls.
Perhaps it is a sparrow or a sandpiper.
Maybe a wren,
echoing its rush-and-jumble song
as it zips through wild berry bushes.

Autumn magic

A cool gush of breeze,
maple leaves sway and clap,
like someone tap dancing,
steal the silence,
then quietly dissolve into oblivion.
All is strangely still.

It comes in again,
a sudden movement of an unseen hand
singing a kind of lullaby to the trees, wordless.

The willows shake their sweeping fronds,
still waters of a pond quiver with fractured reflections,
the sky and the trees, a colorful mosaic.
Leaves skitter and drag
on cemented sun-flecked winding paths.

A sudden rustle,
I catch a squirrel nose-diving
into a pile of crumpled cedar leaves.

The landscape …
painted golden yellow and ochre.

Tread softly

Leaves *crunch*
under a runner's shoes,
leaves that are a crinkled yellow.

It is Fall.
They had their days,
now, they say goodbye to the maple and birch.
pirouetting like ballet dancers before sinking
to the naked ground below.

Leaves *crunch*.
The *crunch* of paper crumpled into a misshapen ball,
thrown like a missile into the garbage bin,
overflowing with paper scribbled a million times over.
Much relief after a hard day's work done.
Maybe frustration that there was still a typo error—
the crunch of another torn sheet, again.

The *crunch* of your teeth
sinking into a crispy nutty granola bar,
unpeeled, mouth drooling.

Lunch forsaken,
in a desperate desire to lose weight,
just digging into a bag of chips.

No luck.

All is not quiet

Plop! plop, droplets of water
from a leaking faucet,
a trickle long neglected,
staining sides of the sink,
its monotonous sound hammering into my head,
till I can take it no more.
Slam the door of the washroom,
block out the noise ... still no respite.

Deafening sounds of a waterfall,
cascading down a rocky precipice
slathered in moss and lichens,
heavy spray of foam bubbles,
exploding into a thousand sparkles,
shining iridescent in the early sunshine.

A rainbow curves across the sky,
      melts into the blue.
    Shadow speckled hillside.

Still waters of a shady summer pond,
shimmer under a straddling maple tree
      soft rustle of its leaves
cascading down, floating on the surface,
creating ripples, concentric circles
becoming bigger and bigger,
swallowed by the sandy bank,
never to return again.

In the setting sun, seagulls cascade down
On cushions of air,
the crash of ocean waves
drowning their hollow cries.

The distant horizon ...
a flash of gold.

A musical interlude

At the far end of the garden,
a summer breeze wafts in,
kisses the cheek and ruffles the hair.
The honeysuckle air, a kind of lullaby,
a shiver of wind ruffling the moment.

At the far end of the garden,
a cacophony of sounds reverberates into the air,
robins, house sparrows and wrens sing in unison
to the *chickadee-dee-dee* of a family of chickadees
pecking at the soft velvety grass under the cherry tree.

A raspy chatter of a magpie echoes the air.
A blackbird dips, flies across,
its wings slicing the air — *Woosh-woosh*.
Far above, the low hum of the airplane,
kite- tailing thin white smoke, as it disappears
into the cloudless blue void.

I was once a child,
just a child trying to catch a cloud,
floating over the garden of my dreams.

A break in the clouds

It is daybreak.
In the distance, gold rimmed, mountains
ring the deep blue sky,

Their peaks, snow slathered
like layers of white paint on a canvas,
ablaze in the first rays of the sun.

Down below, winding lanes
hemmed with cherry trees,
black birds fly low, zoom in,
azaleas, pink fairies with frilly wings dance
in the honeysuckle-laced summer breeze,
as it ruffles their frail petals.

A sudden gust ... *woosh,*
lissome cherry blossoms fill the air,
weightless feathers
afloat in a sea of broken dreams,
fractured realizations,
silhouetted in rings of gold.

A park comes alive

As the evening sun lowers in the horizon
and the sky is a burnished red,
the park comes to life
resounding with cries of children.

Excited whispers, giggles
and shouts of glee
ring into the heavens above,
soft echoes reverberating.

Colorful swings creak,
spiral tube slides bouncing with children.
      They cheer and clap,
        push and get pushed,
the soft sand below .... their mattress.

Mothers watch, glance at their watches,
clap their hands and shout,
        "Its time to go home."
        Who cares?
        Not the children!

An unforgettable summer day

In the afternoon
the sun's fiery flames scorch the earth below.
Miles and miles of sand frame the horizon.
Undulating waves of sand dunes,
rise in a sea , soft and golden,
dotted with palms
that soar into the burnished sky.
the sun, hot and brazen
in a heat dome of blue .

My eyes burn and my throat is parched,
fleshy cactus spikes, pierce the cloudless sky,
    till it bleeds fire.

Beneath a motley copper sky,
burnished and scorched,
I look up, knit my brow,
spot a black spectre, free wheeling far above,
gliding on blazing pillows of air.
Eagle-eyed it waits, its sharp talons
    ready to pounce.
It scours the landscape—a sea of sand,
seamless, pockmarked
with blotches of glassy mirrors,
an oasis, a mirage, an illusion ?

Its shrill haunting whistle
pierces the eerie stillness,
gets louder and louder
till my ear drums almost burst.

A cry of an anguished soul.
It swoops down,
the swish of its wings, draws in air
casts a looming shadow over me...its prey,
like a giant throwing an invisible cape.
I escape into a different world ...
    so serene.

Unfaded memories

In the smouldering skyline of the evening sky,
      swallows fly homewards.

      My shadow lengthens,
galloping across the grass and over the fence.

I watch in silence,
      the rustling of my leaves,
          the only noise,
as the cool night breeze sweeps in.

A family of sparrows settles in their nest,
hastily made of dried leaves, twigs and bracken,
they flap their wings , close their eyes,
lulled by dreams, in their tree home.

I am awake, watching the night sky unravel
its myriad stars and its infinite patterns.

      Soon it will be morning
     and the sun will come
peeping through my lanky branches,
.
There was a time when children
danced and sang under my branches.
They clapped and cheered,
the music of their laughter seeping through me.

      There was a time,
when a mother would sit under my sun dappled shade,
her robotic fingers going clickety-click
     with her knitting needles.

Whisky would come frisking in,
with messy paws and drooling mouth,
yearning for a bite or just a cuddle or pat.
I still remember the little wooden swing
slung on my sturdy branches,

I loved how little Betty giggled,
her floral pink frock flying in the air,
as she almost touched my leaves
with her pudgy little fingers.
How I yearn for those days.

Today, everything is silent and still.
The wind rustles through my bony skeleton,
      sans leaves,
makes a hollow sound, like a lost soul.

The ground below echoes a strange hush,
      there are no children,
no giggles or squeals of excitement.

The creaking swing sits empty,
      the sun sinks lower,
its last rays silhouetting the hazy skyline.

      My shadow,
swallowed by the approaching darkness.

      Past twilight,
only the hum of speeding cars in the distance.

Ocean-scape

Waters lap the shore,
silver sparkles ruffling its bosom.
All the time the one-eyed moon
      watches,
the rhythmic surge of rise and fall of water
      tugging it.

As far as the eye can see,
the frothy sheet, stretches beyond imagination,
swallowed by the inky darkness
hemmed by the twinkling lights of a city,
      so far away.

      Life pulsates there,
  fast and reverberating here.

      The water softly rocks
to the rhythmic sway of the earth and moon,
.
I close my eyes,
draw back the curtain of Time,
see myself driving
down the endless winding prairie highway.

Nothing to see, save flat endless stretches of land
broken by small stretches of shimmering waters.
A glassy brook reflects the scarlet hues of the evening,
hemmed by the bulrushes and the hollow reeds,
      that sing a dirge to the rising wind.

A farm house, a lone sentinel looms in the horizon,
faint lights glimmer in the windows,

Life pulsates.
Inches its way ... slowly.

Spring rain

Grey leaden sky,
broods over a shanty town
draping over low lying wooded hills.
It is a semi-darkness at noon,
the sun blotted by heavy quilted clouds.
The wet starts as a drizzle,
a faint spray that tickles the cheek.
Children play on swings and slides,
unmindful of the rain,
a silvery veil washing over
the newly deserted lanes.

It picks up speed:
pitter-patter, pitter- patter,
drumming on metal roof tops,
like the clatter of horses hoofs on a hot chase.

At other times, it pours.
Buckets of water spill from the sky above,
making the glassy windows tear stained
as my heart bleeds about the past,
the fabric of life, wet
drenched with memories so frayed.

In the stillness of the night

In the stillness of the night,
when everyone sleeps
lulled by dreams of faraway lands,
I lie awake listening to the sounds of emptiness,
nothingness, just mere silence.

All seems quiet, yet, not quiet.
The clock ticks louder, the wind slaps at my window,
makes it rattle, like a ghost knocking, stealthily,
wanting to come in,
a floating figure of the past.

I can hear the rustling of the leaves outside
the rattle of the cherry branch
against my window.

Old Tabby cat shuffles in,
a swish of its furry tail,
Whiskers romps in. bounding,
the thud of his paws, echoing in the darkness.
I can hear him panting, short quick breaths,
shattering the still, warm air of the room.

Everything is silent, and yet ... it is not.

Almost midnight

It is almost midnight,
and all is silent and still.
I hear sounds I was once oblivious to.
I snuggle in my cozy bed,
pull my furry blanket over my ears,
my room is dark, seems quiet,
yet, the house sighs
as if spirits live here.

The musty grandfather clock
hanging in the corner of the living room ticks.
The repetitive tick-tock painful to my ears.

The hinge-less window facing the garden creaks.
I can almost hear the nocturnal wind
Gradually picking up speed.
Leaves of the cedar tree, rustle
to the whim of the midnight wind.

After the rain

A lull,
a hushed silence, a sigh
like when someone is relieved.

The lilies outside my window shed tears of rain,
palm leaves glisten, cleansed of their dust.

The patchy grass wears a washed look,
each blade, a gleaming scimitar.
The maple, almost shorn of its foliage,
stands wet and naked,
A few yellowed leaves, soggy with rain,
still cling to the branches, like nails to a magnet.

The thorny rose bush in the corner,
hangs on to its last bud,
petals unfurled and dank.
Its thin stem bejewelled with raindrops,
that cling, dissolve in the late afternoon.

Down below, the ground is a mesh of weeds
and mossy wild grass
poking out of the squelchy soil.
The pebbled road near the garden,
is awash, damp-mopped and clean.

Autumn wind blows puddles in eddies.
Dried maple leaves skitter at curbside.
Cars drive past leaving behind a spray of fallen rain,
traffic lights reflect a kaleidoscope of color,

The road bleeds red from vehicle tail lights
and green light reflects a florescent hue.
The highway, a glistening mirror,
snaking across the valley,
disappears into nowhere.

Not quite dawn.

The grey sky yawns at the soft approaching light.
the screech of an owl not wanting to waken
echoes in hollow scatters.
The wing flutter of a family of sparrows
takes off at the first gleams of sunlight
filtering through feathery clouds,
awakening an inky black jackdaw,
its soulful cawing, raw and painful …
like salt poured on unhealed wounds.

It is early winter, morning.
A foggy sun winks and blinks
through a canopy of pines and arbutus,
splices through a thick undergrowth
of mossy ferns and wild weeds.

It is strangely quiet, yet the silence
hangs heavy, like a weighted stone.
I hear the flutter of a wing.,
The screech of an owl
echoes through the forest
like an anguished soul
looking for its lost lover.

A creak of a broken twig
sudden footsteps of a tramp, homeless,
the earth his only bed,
the star-lit sky his roof.

Sounds of summer

Summer sun blazes like a torch
scorching the ground below.
The only sound cracking the silence
Is the shrill cry of a eagle
gliding across a pewter sky.

The breeze, laced with smell of honeysuckle,
blows haphazardly but gently,
makes the maple leaves flap and rustle.

Chickadees and house sparrows
play hide and seek in the leafy glen,
the oaks and cedars their home.

Nearby, a stream wends its way
through wild brush and grass,
its gurgling water, a fresh song,

Children bathe in the cool water,
their giggles and laughter
echoing through flickered shadows
of the shady glen.

A furry rabbit, hops from a wild gooseberry bush,
Its woolly tail bobbing and its ears sharp and pointed,
It looks askance, unblinking.

Welcome to my summer abode.

Is it Fall?

Benson mountain rises up,
a salutation to the Fall sky,
puckered with strands of floating clouds.
Lakes shimmer faint stars.
Still waters of hidden brooks
catch the first ripple of autumn breeze.
Their silvery visage mirrors the arbutus and the cedars
like a canvas painting that shimmers
and speaks loud with a muted tongue.

A sea gull soars across the cloudless sky,
enjoys a roller coaster ride on cool cushions of air.

As far as the eye can see,
curvaceous hills arise, painted yellow and sprayed ochre,
with patches of muted greens shaggy willows,
their fronds dancing to the autumn breeze's song.

There is an emotion in the air,
a ragged sense of loss,
as if summer will never return.

Still Autumn

Under a mellow Autumn sun,
rows upon rows of lavender sprigs,
pierce the pristine blue fabric of sky.
A sudden swirl of breeze,
they dance to invisible music from the heavens.
A quiet serenade,
undulating waves of color, dissolving into the ether,
rising, in sync with the cacophony of the buzzing of bees
that hover, as if they have gone tipsy.

The lavender laced air intoxicates me.

Euphoric with delight,
Monarch butterflies flit,
lingering on every sprig
like hummingbirds to a unfurling lily.

The stillness, so hypnotic.

Shimmering brook

Still shimmering brook,
hemmed by tangled blackberry bushes
and bulrushes nodding to the soft murmur of breeze,
the sharp glint of the sun reflects summer.
Near the far end, golden lilies spread cheer.

A still, shimmering brook
sends shivers of tiny ripples
down its watery sheen, as a gentle breeze stirs up,
makes the maple and aspen begin their autumn dance.

The blazing sun, is now mellow.
Yet. it flashes in tiny sparkles that flash and dim.
Blinding luminescence.

The sun sinks low,
squinting behind the wild blueberry bush.
Swallows fly home.
As they sweep across the silky sheen of the sky,
their mercurial shadows flit over pond waters,
to gallop over overgrown furze and fern
pockmarking the grassy valley.

Twilight slips into the abyss of night
as skeins of darkness envelop the island.
A distant star twinkles faintly,
beckons me to its world.

I watch, unblinking.
On the far horizon,
the blue hills are silent,
digesting the remains of the long gone day.

A crescent moon
peeps through a braided cloud.
Pallid moonlight spills over the still pond.

Silence reigns supreme.

Sauntering in the forest

There is a stillness in the air,
strangely quiet,
as if the trees have spoken
and I did not hear
or having heard did not understand.

Maybe it spoke to the Fall fairy
that flits from the arbutus to the fir,
from the cedar to the shaggy dogwood,
touching her magic wand
to every leaf and bush,
till they change color
from endless shades of green
to mellow muted yellows,
giving its clarion call.

The deep blue of the sky,
Is now mottled with clouds
floating like wisps of cotton wool
across the bosom of Mount Benson,
in the far horizon.

On the other side,
lies the ocean,
an ultramarine sheet of water,
a shimmering mirror
dissolving into the pale blue mountain ranges,
so lofty and sacred.

Dawn awaits

Quiet as a mole,
a faint light steals through a veil of cloud,
unwrapping the darkness of the night.

It is morning, still and sombre,
not a sound is heard.

A breeze stirs up, the air
laced with the smell of lavender
growing wild and carefree.

A thrush springs from the over-grown grass,
smells the day, nose dives back
into the shivering blades of sage leaves
and is seen no more.

Rosy glow of a slick dawn
gently fans across the cloud peppered sky,
the landscape bathed in luminous light,
as if there was never night.

A high tide of starlings rolls in,
silhouettes of gold,
dips low and as if taking a bow,
soars   into oblivion.

The early hour

Early morning,
slow stirring of today's chores
as sleep still lingers,
snug under a veil of heavy mist,
a translucent cloak over the town.

The darkness of the night refusing to leave,
even when the pale light of dawn beckons in the east.
Soft gush and whoosh of a cool breeze
makes the juniper and the pine stir awake
sending a shiver through their spines.

    I am a runner chugging uphill,
panting , every breath an act pf labor.

    Heavy footsteps,
the uphill climb swallowed in swirling mist
that wraps around the cedar trees
their jagged outline somewhat visible
    on the horizon.

Maybe I am a homeless vagabond,
    a nomad, a gypsy.

My bed is the soft ground below,
my food the sun-burst berries from the wild bush,
I drink water from the spring
spouting from the depths of the earth ,
fresh breeze of the ocean fills my lungs.
My family is a pair of sparrows
nesting in the lower branch of the arbutus.

The star spangled night sky watches over me,
    as the night rocks me to sleep.

    Maybe I am an old man
    shuffling with faltering footsteps,

My lungs almost collapsing,
chugging uphill like a slow moving train.
My cheeks are blushed red,
      a wisp of grey hair
limp on my receding forehead.

I have travelled many a milestone,
raised a family, slogged at my work,
now it is time to take things easy.

Let me live in this moment,
watch the mist-wrapped landscape
like a bird scans the frosty valley below.

      I am a child walking to school,
        my eyes filled with hope ,
fresh as a dewdrop reflecting the baby blue sky,
        smiling back at me.

Winter beckons

It is not quite morning.
Drawing my bedroom window curtain,
I see snowflakes falling,
      pirouetting,
dancing like damsels in the semi-dark,
confetti from above,
celebrating the newborn day
—the first breath of dawn—
      still and silent.

It has been snowing for awhile.
Our backyard still sleeps
under a blanket of white,
The rhododendrons
bend low under clumps of fresh snow,
like giant whipped meringues skillfully crafted,
silent sentinels of wintry days arriving..

Just around the corner,
I see rows upon rows of cottages,
their roofs pockmarked with snow.

Sounds of silence

In the silence of the night,
I draw aside the curtain
and peer through my bedroom window.

There is silence.

Street lights shine
on a steady stream of fine snowflakes,
confetti dropping from above.
A fine spray of sparkling luminescence,
mesmerizes all who watch,
including the old feathery horned owl
that holds vigil late into the night,
night that gently rocks the world to sleep.

The landscape, a patchwork of stark maple branches
a filigree of entwined veins coursing the sombre sky,
are like broken tuning forks
swaying to the rhythm of a sudden breeze,
starting from the east.

The sky, a pale grey,
speaks to the cypress trees frosted with snow,
standing like freshly whipped meringues
ready to be licked by the Arctic breeze.

We sleep, warm and snug,
lulled by soft dreams of tropical climates,
of blue tranquil seas that lap the golden sands
of palm dotted beaches.

Outside my window,
the wind picks up speed,
strong flurries sweep across ,
picking up snow, like chaff,
a *swirling dervish* in a trance.
The night stretches long and dark.

Just Passing By

No sound
except the cry of a coyote,
the sudden flutter of a nightjar's wing
and the occasional hoot of an old barn owl,
that has seen too many winters.

The night slips into the wee hours of the morning,
    I peep through my laced window
        breathless,
      watching the first streaks of light
     stretch across the pale moonlight
        that still lingers.

    The first breath of dawn.

Au revoir

The sky casts its rosy evening hue
from lavender to a misty mauve.
The sun has long since said goodbye
to the evening and the white quilted winter valley
dotted with solitary farmsteads
and spout swirls of smoke from chimneys.

Skeins of twilight flicker over clumps of snow
clinging to the speckled conifers and firs.
Shadows limp over the white mantle,
that once resembled our usual yard,
Our herb pots wear mystical shapes,
sculpted by the frigid arctic wind.

Outside,
there is a void,
a hushed silence and the longing to hear
the swish of the breeze,
the rustle of dry snow floating down
from branches of soaring pines,
a longing to hear
the gurgling waters of the brook,
the swish of someone's rain boots
plodding through knee deep snow,
the scrape of a shovel against the cobbled road,
the laughter of kids,
tobogganing down a snowy slope,
as their laughter echoes through the pines
sighing heavy under clumps of snow.

Where am I in all this?
Just a number?
A mere cog in the wheel of the Universe?

Winter has come and will give way to Spring.
Time flows on like a river with no destination,
I watch and bear witness ... tongue-tied.

A night to remember

Cold moon,
a frigid December moon,
barren and sallow,
eerie and pale,
breathtaking.

Stars burn in the dark cavern of the night.
Pale moonlight glimmers, then spills,
peeping through snow -crusted cypress boughs,
to dance on the white quilted landscape
shimmering silver.

Shadows gallop across,
the raw air that has no weight,
They talk to the arbutus,
sweep across the frost rimmed brook
pricked by the North star.

The silence is deafening.
Someone seems to call,
yet there is no sound.

Maybe an echo of the past
that had no beginning ...
no end.

Frayed memories

I look at the photograph,
the one in a silver frame and fluted edges.
It is rich with memories of the past,
mellow and nostalgic.

I run my fingers over her face,
so gentle and serene
like soft moonlight on a cloudless night.

Her lips, like fluted petals,
uncurl to say a silent prayer,
soothing to a troubled mind.

At other times they break into a smile
that lights up my whole world.

Her eyes, soft and deep,
speak many a word
even when none is spoken.

At other times,
they are shallow pools of emotion,

You laughed a lot, with your eyes,
although you are speechless now,
only to hear my laughter
echoing throughout the room.

I walked in your shadow
for years as we walked together,
your arm around me,
like to two bosom friends.
Sometimes hand in hand.

We braved many a storm,
when life's journey became tortuous.
We shed tears of laughter
and sauntered through valleys,

blooming with lilies,
their fragrance alluring.

We danced around still ponds,
hemmed with bulrushes.

Never would not tread those paths again.

They have gone,
gone like a whispering wind
caressing the last leaf
that still clings to the old oak tree.

I shall never forget you,
dear mother,
my very flesh and bone.

Resilience

      What am I?
      Who am I?

A puny creature with a fist-size heart?
A giant microcosm of cells
working in spilt-second precision?
A body of electrical charges
and countless nerve impulses firing non-stop?

Am I an engineered structure of skin and bone
with microscopic tubes coursing through it,
all programmed and remotely timed,
to run its course or vanish into the blue,
like a candle in the wind?

      Wait a minute,
You can call me puny, call me fragile,
but I am much more than that.
I am a reservoir of strength.
I am a mountain peak
that faces blinding blizzards,
lashing winds.
I remain unscathed.
because I am strong.

    I am that trickle of water
that drips down softly and steadily,
never giving up,
till I become a thunderous waterfall
that can tear through rocks
and chisel granite.

      I am that tiny seed,
        half-buried under gravel,
that has not seen the light of the day,
yet is able to rise,
to break through the hard crusty soil,
its tender leaves curling to breathe new life.

You can call me puny, call me fragile,
yet my spirit remains unvanquished.
     Never giving up,
because the sun always shines through
no matter how menacing the clouds are.
I will overcome the unexpected and face the storm
till it dies down.

     I am a boat
that crosses unchartered angry seas,
spilling with lashing waters and giant waves,
     yet I sail on.

There are many moments
when my boat rocks so hard
   that it almost overturns,
and becomes a smashed matchbox.

When the wind blows me away,
I will adapt my sails to it.
I will never give up.
I will not just jump puddles
I will cross oceans even
when there is no land to see.
I will get up,
even when I have fallen many a time.
because I have ... resilience.

Water's edge

I stand at the edge of a stream.
Its waters flow slowly,
never stopping, like a magnetic pull by an unseen force.
Its ripples and gurgling, music to my ears.

In the distant, a hazy horizon stretches
outlined by mist wrapped conifers.
Tall willows, with their fronds swaying,
almost sweeping the mercurial surface,
hem the stream , as if protecting it from losing its way
as it snakes and loops towards the setting sun.

I look below, my face mirrored in the shimmering water,
blurred with the lengthening shadows of the willows
that crisscross their hazy reflections.
I watch a giant painting of trees
and a stream wending its way,
the canvas sky, a perfect marine blue
with swatches of fluffy clouds,
the green and pale yellow slathered on the trees.
A perfect mix melding into the stream.

There is not a sound to be heard,
except the gush of water
quenching my thirsty soul.
The sun hides behind a smouldering red cloud
and a wing burst of sparrows
dives low towards the stream,
missing me by inches.

A hummingbird takes flight,
its wings a blur,
a marvel in motion,
soon beyond oblivion.

Time slows down,
but never stops.

The path still untrodden

I walk on a mud-rutted path
snaking towards a forest.
It seems to be leading nowhere.
Do I follow it?

Maybe it leads to a stream.
Maybe it is swallowed by the dense fir trees.

I wonder.
Is it the same with life?

I wonder where Life will take me,
which road should I follow?
When will the next milestone appear?
Will it appear at all?

The journey so far, has been long,
yet exciting,

I have seen many faces,
faces that have become bosom friends,
Others have turned strangers,
pretend they did not know me
when our lives were interwoven together.

We follow a bell shaped curve.

A tiny bud uncurls,
its petals silky and soft,
the first kiss of dawn and it unfurls like a flag,
a blooming lily, trumpeting the world,
'please stop and smell me'.

None stop, except the hummingbird.

From a scraggly stem, a sap green leaf
gingerly peeps into an aligned world,
morning sun rays embracing its soft contours.

Encrusted with morning dew,
the soft green blade of the leaf
reflects the day.

Dawn slips into dusk and Time slips by,
the leaf turns limp, then yellow,
sinks into the ground below ,
to sleep forever.

It is the same with Life.

We play our role
and when it is curtain call,
we take a final bow.
and fade into oblivion.

Silence speaks

The room at the far end is empty,
the cushioned chair as you left it.
A half- drooping lily sheds tears in the blue vase.
The silence haunts me.
The door creaks,
as a cold gust of breeze sweeps across the yard
making the sole window, rattle.

The fireplace is cold
with dying embers of woody ash,
of a past freshly buried,
the pain still lingers,
snuffing out the future.

I hear your voice,
soft and soothing,
changing into a slur.
Your body like a sack of potatoes,
slips into an abyss,
bottomless,
and then you are gone.

I drown in a whirlpool of tears,
sucked into Nothingness.

Something nudges me to rise,
not to let Life drift away into oblivion,
to bring it ashore where the sun shines bright
and Hope lives eternal.

The ebb and tide of memories

Snow drizzled mountains rise
above a furry carpet of conifers and pines,
among rolling glades and rocky creeks.
The sky is a deep blue, like lapis lazuli,
the noon sun blinks at the shimmering ocean,
its waves lap the sandy beach
dimpled with footprints of children who have gone,
tucking away memories of salty waters
and melt-in-the mouth sundaes.

A few moss encrusted logs
lie strewn across scattered sea shells,
reminders of last year's storm aftermath.
Summer breeze blows, eases and waits,
as if to hear the prattle of a wren
that has lost its way to its nest
tucked away behind a shady cove.

Sometimes, a shrill cry of an eagle, haunting,
echoes across the endless stretch of blue,
then into the blurred horizon,
where sea and sky become one.

Memories rise and crash land in my mind,
exploding the past into smithereens ...

A past that never existed.

The magic hour

In the fading rays of the setting sun,
I watch the poplars and the firs silhouetted in gold
as they rise above the slated roofs of cottages
dotting the island.

Dusky light peeps through the filigree
of conifer branches lining the solitary roads.
A few cars drive by as the day is done.

It is time for morning vespers.
Church spires gleam in the distance,
a bell echoes across the silent valley
swaddled in the approaching evening mist
arising from the west.

I gaze into the distance:
The sky is a smouldering ball of fire,
smudged with wispy clouds.
The soft breeze sings a dirge to the dying day.
Swallows swoop low, warblers chatter
their notes rise into the blue.

Something happens...quiet as a feather,
the wind eases and waits.
The prattle of the birds falls silent.
Leaves dance softly.
The river meanders slower.
The sun sinks lower and lower.
The day wanes into no man's land ...
neither dusk nor dawn.
Silence reigns in the hallowed realm of a world
swathed in mystic purple hues.
It is twilight ... Neither day nor night.

The scythe figure of pallid moon, faintly visible.

The evening star, late in coming.

Flying high

Drawing the frilly lace curtain of my window,
I look up at a speckled canvas of sky,
dabbed with little blobs of white cottony clouds,
floating in a sea of deep blue.

I see the clouds in slow motion,
not a care in the world,
where are they going?
To a destination unknown to them?
Or towards me, beckoning me to their world?

Wish I was a cloud,
I would not have to slog and study,
not have to pour over anthologies and doctrines,
till every cell in my brain is hyper-saturated.

I blink ...
I am sure I saw three bears strutting across the sky,
papa, mama and little baby bear!
Was I dreaming ? Was it just an illusion?
Maybe I had read too much of *Goldilocks*?
Maybe my imagination was playing tricks.

I blink again,
rub my eyes with my tiny palm,
see a beautiful chariot,
afloat in lapis lazuli waters,
rocked gently by the lullaby of the breeze,
a dream slowly vanishing into the blue.

The sun has long gone,
velvety darkness waits in the wings
of tall cypress trees
sighing to the breeze that stirs up
from the distant lair of the ocean.

A bustling stressed out day
crawls to a slow stop.

People put their pens down,
switch off computer screens
with a deep sigh of relief,
rub their tired eyes,
wave a hurried goodbye to their colleagues,
stomp out of their cubby holes.

      Aaah!
A breath of fresh air.

Let us float among the clouds.

A pond comes alive

I sit on the grassy ledge
overlooking the pond hidden by tall bulrushes,
that sway like lissome dancers in the breeze.
        Its waters, a shimmering mirror
        that soak up the morning sun.

Come night,
        it is a star-glittered platter.

The water is not too deep,
easy to peer down to its pebbled bottom,
speckled with seaweeds and mossy ferns,
home to tiny fish and the squirmy aquatic world
swarming aimlessly, looping in and out.

Occasionally my wandering eye
catches a glimpse of a tiny squiggly fish,
lurking near its slippery banks.

Late night breeze starts up,
creating ripples on surface of the pond,
as if it is a live thing shivering.

On an impulse my hand reaches out
to a round, speckled pebble
hidden beside the mossy grass.
I throw it across and into the still pond.
It comes to life, the quiet of the night shattered,

Placid waters break into a thousand ripples,
little concentric circles become bigger and bigger
kissing the weedy shore,
        then they disappear,
             into total nothingness.

I ponder, is not my life, a circle in motion
like the silent movement of the galaxies?
And the planets that swirl around them?

Just Passing By

Nothing happens in a hurry,
Time, like a well oiled machine,
is programmed to the very minute,
to the very millisecond.

Seasons change
from the resurgence of Spring
to sultry summer days,
followed by the crazy dance of Fall.

Finally
        comes the mystic silence of winter.

I have travelled many a milestone,
a helpless baby, then a naughty girl
playing pranks at every step.

Childhood quickly slipped into youth,
when roses seemed to have no thorns.
The world was a fragrant, blooming garden,
but in mid-life it was not so.

Then came a milestone where Time stood still,
children left home, echoes of their voices faded.
My mind became an empty shell,
retracting into a cocoon of memories,

The 'plop' of the pebble slipping into the water
wakes me from my reverie.
A gentle breeze stirs up,
rustles through the maple leaves.
        sends them scurrying.

I watch a black furry squirrel
        frisk past me,

I hear the flapping of wings
near a bramble bush,
The shrill cry of a lone eagle

shatters the silence.
Low hum of a car speeding on a highway,
	not far off

		reminds me of home.

Back *to terra firma.*

What does a mountain say?

Mount Benson rises in front of me,
its soft fur of cypress and cedar,
gently outlining its sloping contours.
Tiny houses dot its base,
the ocean a sheet of mercurial water,

Mount Benson rises in front of me,
knobbed with freshly drizzled snow
It is the first frost dusting, speckling its visage,
that looks like crumpled velvet,
under a canopy of grey clouds that augurs more snow,
    falling like dandruff,
        dreaming of sunny days.

Mount Benson rises in front of me.
    The day dawns to an azure sky,
        No clouds in sight,
except for a few high clouds straddling like wispy cotton
    that float aimlessly.

The sun is high up in the sky,
its rays silhouetted on its ridge.
The gentle veil of morning mist lifts gradually,
a wing flutter of sparrows and chickadees
fills the early morning stillness.

Mount Benson rises in front of me.
It is afternoon
    and the sun is high up in the sky.
A shadow shivers over the mountain,
    a golden eagle swoops low,
        playing on cushions of air,
    as it glides and twirls like a trapeze artist.

Far away, roofs of ranches and cottages
gleam in the sunshine,
snug in the lap of the mountain.

Mount Benson rises in front of me.
The setting sun deepening in the sunlight
    before it says goodbye
and a cool gust of breeze stirs up.

Low lying hills are still bathed in the mellow light
as the west shimmers and distant clouds dance
to the slosh of waves.

Seagulls glide on cushions of air.
    All is cloaked in silence.

There was a time

Life is a mosaic
patched with happiness
that spreads its colors so luminous
as blues of sorrow rise and fall
into the bottomless pits of that blue sorrow,

At other times,
I feel like an innocent doe
sauntering in a quiet shadow-flecked glade.

There was a time,
when Life was a garden,
fragrant and blooming
with roses and lilies always.

Little did I realize
that it would become
an overgrowth of wild bramble bushes,

Now there remain only prickly thorns
That make my heart bleed.

There was a time
when Life was all fun and frolic.
A few curveballs thrown at me, jolted me awake,

I realize now,
Life is not just a piece of clay
to be moulded into a dumb doll.
It is more precious than a Dresden China doll
and should be treated as such ...
most precious indeed.

Sleeping under the stars

Unfolding my sleeping bed,
I rest my head on the soft grassy patch
overlooking a low lying hill.

Mother earth's lap
rocking a gentle lullaby
with its rhythmic motion in the vast inky void.

Here I am, gazing at a dark, star spangled sky
        brooding over me.

It is strangely quiet,
      the silence captivating,
           yet, the silvery blush of stars
be it the Great Bear constellation or the Ursa Minor,
      or maybe the Andromeda,
seem to beckon me to another world,
a world that is so far, yet so close.
It feels like it's a part of my heart beat,
      my very breath.

I see myself sucked in a whirlpool of blushing stars,
      to dissolve into thin air.

      A soft breeze stirs up,
rocking the earth like a giant cradle,
a rustle in a nearby bramble bush.
      Maybe a wild rabbit
  weary after a late night chase.

A bird calls, perhaps a wren,
in unison with the haunting hoot of an owl
hiding among the lowly branches of an oak tree,
the echo permeates the silent valley.

      I take a deep breath,
  the cool air has a faint scent,
maybe reminiscent of honeysuckle or wild rose,

Just Passing By

I feel the soft velvety grass
with the palms of my hands,
    I close my eyes,
my heart beats and the earth pulsates
    in sync.

    We are part of a whole.
    The whole, a part of us.
      Binding humanity.

Here I lie
on the soft bed of the earth
    choked no more
between draperies and walls,
    an escape from the bastille
      of civilization.

    I may have dozed off,
then something made me open my eyes.,
    I know not what.

The nightly darkness had melted away,
giving way to a faint glimmer of light in the east.
    Somewhere deep in the valley,
      the shrill cry of a cock
      came like a cheerful watchman,
        counting the hours to dawn.

I look upwards,
a few stars still shine faintly
in the somewhat grey firmament.

It is daybreak.
It is time for woolly sheep in the meadows
to break their fast,
for the cattle to awaken,
for the world to get back to the grind of Life,
while I listen to the silent symphony
    of the fading stars,

soaring to the heavens above ...

   'tis the magical hour.

Blue on blue

        Outside my window,
  the city lies before me, blinking.
Bright flickering lights splashed across
        the palate of the island.

        Then there is the blue sea,
      deep and rich, overflowing,
  tears and emotions rising and falling,
      swelling in a bottomless pit.

 Lapis lazuli waters melt
to kiss the baby blue of the mountains
      swaddled in morning mist,
their craggy peaks crusted with snow
      glinting an opal white
  in the blinding glare of the sun.

      An image calls
from the blurry precipice of my memory

      — those days —

when I would hold your hand,
        dear mother
  and walk through ankle deep snow
        up in the mountains,
and make a snowman
      with a carrot as its nose.
Our laughter piercing the stillness.

Gone are those days,
      yes they are gone.

All that remains
        is a jagged piece
            of a jigsaw puzzle,
      a part of a chequered mosaic
        we call Life.

All is quiet.

      The silence rises
           like a wave engulfing me.

Passing by — a detour

Just passing by,
I stumbled on a stockpile of memories,
musty and long forgotten,
bringing back stinging tears that cannot be washed away,
no matter how I try.

    Others,
that are sweet and unforgettable
        linger
  like the smell of lavender,
drowning me in a sea of euphoria,
    dog eared with doting love.

Need I go through them?

The long and winding passage of Time.
    It seems an endless journey.

I have crossed many milestones,
      hit numerous barriers and bumps
           only to get wiser by the day.

Just passing by,
      run my hands over a picture,
          faded and mellow with age.
That dimpled smile and twinkle in your eyes,
      speaks volumes to me.
The past unravels in muted silence.

Just passing by,
      I met the poetic Muse,
was inspired to juggle a few words
      to make a tapestry of poems,
          perchance a passerby would read it.

Just passing by,
    met lovely people
    who became friends,

bonded like siblings,
stitched Life's strands together
　　　then left me suddenly,
　　　　vanishing into the blue.

I crossed another milestone,

　　　　I still have miles to go.
　　　before the journey ends

Author Profile — Kamal Parmar

Poet and writer from Vancouver Island, Kamal has been passionately involved in writing since high school and University years. Her genre is poetry and creative non-fiction. Her poems are simple, though poised and evocative enough to set the reader thinking. She has a few books published in UK, Canada and India and many publications in reputed US and Canadian literary journals and anthologies. Her writings have won many honorable mentions and prizes.

Kamal has been a member of a several writers organizations and Writers Guilds. She was an active member of Saskatchewan Writers Guild , for many years and also a voluntary peer reviewer with the Manitoba Writers organisation. Currently, she is an Associate member of the *League of Canadian Poets* and a Board member of the *Federation of BC writers.* She is also a member of *Haiku Canada*, a member of the *Canadian Authors Association* and of *The Writers Union of Canada* with whom she is a voluntary peer reviewer, screening poetry manuscripts of self-published writers. She is also a past Board member of Nanaimo Arts Council. She is the current Poet Laureate of the City of Nanaimo.

www.ingramcontent.com/pod-product-compliance
Lightning Source LLC
Chambersburg PA
CBHW070337120526
44590CB00017B/2922